Coffee Induced Mumbling

Transient

Loud Dreams

PRESS

Printed in Canada

First printing, 2016

Second Edition

ISBN 978-0-9952673-1-2

Loud Dreams Press

www.louddreamspress.com

Dedicated to

Gaganjit Bassi, may you never be forgotten.

&

for Kay, may your words continue to rattle the stages, glisten the pages and

moisten the hearts.

Roadmance

You say I'm yours.
Maybe I am.
Maybe, I was but you —
You were never mine.

I am a bench,
a resting place
shade from the sun
but she,
she is home and people
always return home.

Maybe all roads lead back to this,

back to you.

I keep trying to paint new portraits elsewhere.

The same colors keep bleeding.

The same void keeps weeping, like an inconsolable child.

This, stubborn love keeps speaking, and maybe

I'm in need of a lifeline.

I hope it's still you on the other side.

- Us

Promise

When I nick named you after a vegetable.

When you couldn't stop laughing.

When you said you couldn't handle spice but for me, you'd sweat through it.

When you taught me your lingo.

When you started using mine.

When you told me they say you look like your old man, promising never to become him.

When I swore I'd never be like mine.

When I said I was naming all of our children, you laughed and asked to name just one.

I said you'd get a middle name.

When I broke your heart.

When you picked up mine.

When you said I love you.

When I said goodbye.

Maybe I'll see you at "one day",

where broken promises live.

This thing called love

It still lingers.

Floats around like an afterthought,

a favorite memory,

a shared joke.

Neither of us laugh now.

Lying next to you—

Still wearing me

- The morning after

Truth is

Sometimes I wonder,

is it you that I miss or what we could have been.

The dreams we carved on to tree trunks,

promises whispered on leaves.

It's complicated

I am in love with you.
Completely, utterly smitten.

Sometimes I'm a torrent.
You, are white water rafting and I am going the wrong direction.

We are not always treading the same plot lines but you
are always a part of my story—
leading role even when you antagonize me.

Sometimes you stare at me like a blank page and I am
a procrastinating student typing bullshit with one hand,
clenched coffee mug with the other.

Sometimes you are Eden and I am unholy.
My tears unworthy of watering your seeds but your tree,
is always an attentive ear, catching every word as
I whisper my dreams.

Sometimes you're a seamstress, quilting my stories, patching me up

along the way.

Sometimes you are my mother, scolding me, why can't you do better?

Sometimes you are my father, abandoning me and then asking where

I have been.

I, have been here all along.

Sometimes I am my father, I leave you and then demand to know where

you have been.

You, are still here.

You excite me like holding concert tickets.

You are the first snowfall of winter.

We are ice storms.

We are blackouts.

You are always there for my icicles,

my black outs, when I'm too cold to write

when I black out, all the things I don't want to remember.

You insist.

Stubborn you are.

Like a teething child you cause me pain.

You pull out, pain,

like lovers not wanting to use condoms.

You challenge me,

shelter me.

Here's to you.

Blank page.

Spilled ink.

Holder of secrets.

You, are teaching me

to love too.

To love me,

like you do.

Sometimes, it still hurts
all at once and that's okay.

- Healing

Unsent letters

Dear Piccadilly Circus,

I still fancy your name, don't ask me why, I just do.

Dear random coffee shop,

your coffee was deplorable, diabolical and depraved but your

owner was amused by my Canadian accent, I'll let you slide.

Dear Westfield Shopping Center,

with all your attractions indoors my gaze shifted to the main
event outside.

Old boy suited up asked me for a lighter and ignited more than
cigarette.

Dear Sheppard's Bush,

your proximity to the mall impressed me, I'm enamored by
convenience.

Dear Hyde Park,

I've witnessed prayers completed in your presence at a time I
was haunted by absence.

Its ghosts still linger, tantalizing me with mirages of what ifs and
what could have beens.

I hope to return one day and water you with my tears.

For in that there is mercy, in that there is truth.

The truth our lips dare not speak.

So we weep, and weep.

Dear London Eye,

At your highest of heights I found common ground.

Somewhere along the way, I lost it.

Maybe one day your pinnacle can bring me down to earth.

Dear Oxford street,

I've been thinking of you.

I've, contemplated reuniting with you.

Your pavement can match my cinder block façade,

how does one not harden in the labyrinth of a concrete jungle?

Dear Big Ben,

They say time heals all wounds, how much longer?

Dear London Bridge,

How does one let go when they know they should?

How does one let go when they know they shouldn't?

Dear Piccadilly Circus,

I've been on the verge of coming to you.

My stone like heart talked me off the ledge.

I'm glad, it wouldn't be fair.

You continue to inspire my work as if you're holding the pen

while the ink free falls on the pages.

Maybe one day we'll drench the pages together.

Dear Piccadilly Circus,

I know you're multilingual,

I wonder

do you speak broken?

Can you decipher hurt?

Will you translate struggling?

I hear it's universal.

Kinda, Sorta, Black

I feel like you should beat box or like
dance for the talent show.
Huh? What you talking about Willis?
I'm as perplexed as sweet brown was
when she woke up for that cold pop and
discovered Lord it's a fire!

And now I'm having this whole dialogue in
my head like what does she take this for,
what was she expecting?
Does she think that upon exiting the
womb we don't come out crying, instead
we come out making wonderful beat
boxing noises like

Nope, not me, I guess my mother missed
those essential cool vitamins.
I subdue the inner flames that comment
ignites, because an eruption?
Ain't nobody got time for that.

Why do you think I should beat box
or like dance, is it because I'm black?
Well, yeah
but you're like kinda, sorta, black.

Kinda, sorta, black?
I mean you speak so well and like you
don't even have an accent.
Um, thanks, I guess, neither do you.
Did you forget you immigrated too?
I can see why you're confused.
Tell a lie long enough and you'll start to
believe it's the truth.

And you use all these big words, like
your vocab is so...big
Well you see I have this thing for words
and there's this place that's full of them
along with their meanings, it's called
dictionary.com you should check it out.

Okay okay okay so you're like black right.
What's up with this black lives matter
hashtag, I mean all lives matter right?
Right?
They say orange is the new black
but you never hear of any attacks for being
orange.
You're too black for them and not black
enough for them
do you see where dilemma stems?

From being neither here nor there
as they awkwardly stare
I can see their brains grinding
trying to figure me out.

If a cop pulls me over will he be blinded by
my "lightness" or will I be deafened by the
sound of his trigger pulling?
Riddle me that
and then tell me that I'm just "kinda, sorta,
black".

We're trying to unshackle ourselves from
chains they insist don't exist.
Shattering invisible glass ceilings
underneath the glass ceiling.

Sterling said what makes you think you can
coach them?
But Willie answered it best.
He taught you how to tame them —

15

Use their differences against them.
Keep some indoors.
Treat them slightly better.

Voilà
that's how you stew self hate.
#winning
#teamlightskin
#redbone
#yellabone
#lookingforabadyella

Shabazz signed with X.
Nothing good comes before it and what
comes after it is confusion.

Example
ex-spouse
ex-terminate
which is what they want to do to us.

TrayvonX'd.
Mike X'd.
Sandra, Laquan, JamarX'd.

Rachel, x'd.
Oops, nope that's just the box she marks
whenever she thinks it's convenient to black.
When is it ever convenient to be black?
When is it, ever, convenient, to be black?
She's still kicking, hasn't gagged on her
privilege yet
I guess that's the gag.

Y
Why do you bury evidence?
It's evident you'll be acquitted anyway.
That's even if you even get indicted.
Why'd you break Freddie's neck?

Was it to make Sandra spineless?
Silly rabbit, don't you know tricks are for
kids?
Just call a spade a spade
And spell it out for us
Suicide —
I mean murder.
He resisted arrest —
We just wanted a punching bag.
She gave attitude —
How dare she stand up for herself.

                    Oh God, not another black lives matter
                                                    piece.
                        Yes, another one jerk off
                    because black lives do matter.
                        And yeah all lives matter.
                        Even yours prick, we know.
        The value of your lives was never up for
                            debate, you made sure of it.

Stop criticizing how we mourn.
Better yet stop giving us reasons to.
But hey, what do I know?
I'm just "kinda, sorta, black".

Ten things to the younger me

One

Curly bangs, girl no. I know you love them but girl, no.

Two

When you get wasted for the first time, try to come up with a better excuse for puking your guts out than, I had a really bad donut.

Your teachers will not believe you.

Your misery will invade their nostrils like pancake batter on weekends.

Three

When your friend tells you about her gang do not ask to join.

When she tells you about the perks, do not be obviously interested.

When she finally tells you how to get in,

the greatest words that will ever leave your mouth are

girl I don't know about all that,

I kind of like my face.

Four

Bassi will die.

It'll hurt.

You will hate your friend for how she told you.

You will hate flowers.

You will hate your hands for trembling while placing the petals in his casket.

You will hate the casket.

You will want it to be gentle with your boy.

You will loathe your fingers for not calling him.

You will loathe your fingers for calling him, after he is gone.

You will remove all of his pictures,

you won't be able to look at the them but you won't let

his memory fade.

You will hug bottles.

Bottles will surround you like a business of ferret.

A Parliament of owls.

A murder of crows.

An unkindness of ravens.

You will be unkind to yourself.

One day, learn, to forgive yourself.

Five

When your half sister emails you, do not reply.

She will be alluring like do not push buttons, like foreign accents.

She will sew new buttons on you.

You will press eject when you finally realize that she will always be more

his daughter than she could ever be

your sister.

Six

The first time you are called turban head, you will not know what a turban is.

It'll be confusing like visiting your grandmother and her not knowing who you are.

No, your hijab is not a turban.

Seven

An old lady at the football game will yell "you people are all the same".

You will leap from the bleachers and want to square up.

Yeah, you're pissed.

Yeah you want to beat her with her own cane.

Relax.

That's somebody's grandma.

A racist hag?

Sure, but somebody's grandma.

Eight

When your mother asks you why your eyes are bloodshot red, tell her it's

from all the crying after the latest whack the piñata she played with your body.

She will believe you.

Nine

When your mother tells you you only beat the ones you love, do not believe her.

She does not love you.

That is not love.

She will mistake you for a horse, she will try to beat submission into you.

You will not bow down.

You will wear bruises like a favorite sweater that won't keep you warm.

You will curse your skin.

This lightness they praise you for will carry a stench of omen.

You will become more dubious than Thomas.

More crucifixion than second coming.

More Psalms of David, your whimpers will become hymn.

More David without the kingdom.

More David without the sling shot.

You are not David.

She is not Goliath.

Do not hit her.

You have never hit her.

You will hit the walls.

You will hit yourself.

You will take another hit.

You will take another shot—

Bastard.

She takes another shot.

Ten

Chin up.

You will leave.

She will never mark your body again.

She will never extract your crimson again.

You will vow,

you, will never be a monster.

You,

will never be her.

Fragments

When she looks at me, all she sees is him.

Broken,

promises

heart

pieces

I was born into the madness the fragments.

When she looks at me, all she sees is him.

And I know she says it to stab me to harm me

every time she yells you're just like him.

And every time she calls me his daughter,

the words, pierce through me

like a dagger as I try to dodge her fury staggering out the door.

And every time I walk away, I become more his daughter as my
back faces her.

When.

When did I sign up to become my father's keeper?

The atoner of his sins.

This.

        This
    is   not
        a
    cross
        I
    chose
    to bear.

This crown, was not the one I had envisioned.

These

thorns

weaved around my head do not make me selfless.

For I, did not choose to carry his sins.

I am not salvation and I refuse

to let these lashes paint me victim.

I have no cheeks left to turn for they,

have been bloody for far too long.

This crown

does not make me martyr.

I am not Messiah but

he

wears Judas

so

damn

well.

Tunnel

Optimism becomes more obscene,
more absurd.

Frigid, frozen, fragile like skating on a pond.

Hopes doomed hopeless.
Bodies held soulless.

The man jumps the train tracks.
The passengers scream.

Plastered pieces,
obliterated life.

All they see,
The derailed train derailing their plans.

Origins

My father's name is Adam.
As in leaving.
As in original sin.
As in the one I've been paying for ever since —
The beginning.

Genesis.
My mother stays bent like the rib she was made from.
Afraid of her snapping so I branched off.
I lost concern for her mental health.

I find myself still burning from her mental hell.
Scorching like a summer's day,
praying for the night breeze.
Sleep cludes me as my tears heave.

My half sister invades my dreams.
I lay down my arms.
I hold her hand, the moment.
She speaks five languages and her tongue still doesn't grasp me.

I wonder if she knows I refer to her as friend.
As in not kin.
As in we do not bleed the same.
She does not bleed red,
she bleeds him.

As in poster child.

As in chosen one.

As in next line.

I do not wish for the deed to his crown.

The one of thorns fits me well.

As in it's my size.

As in Messiah didn't have a father too.

I asked Adam for a paternity test.

I wonder if he was insulted by the question, or afraid of the
answer.

I too, am afraid.

I'm unsure which frightens me more,

finding out that I've been hating the wrong person

or solidifying that it was

the right one

all along.

Open

I may have sprung you into life.

Illustrated you in my daydreams, traced

your outline on my train of thought.

Spoke your cadence on my tongue,

felt your goosebumps on my spine.

Melted in your derailing stride,

as if I was a snowflake on your palm.

We've always been, more storm than calm.

And now you're gone.

I sketched you in my daydreams,

in my night terrors you'll live on.

Neptune

She is a torrent.
Pulling me in.
Around and around.

Stuck.
A cycle.
A song on repeat.

We keep looping,
scratching.
Broken,
record.
We've broken,
records.

Deafening argument number?
I've lost count.
I keep counting ways to leave,
to end it.
She keeps spitting up reasons to hold me captive.

Doesn't she know that fireflies were made
to light up the sky?

Doesn't she know that I was made to light up
the hearts?
That I do not need a pair to be saved.

That there is only one of me and I will

not drown.

That I've already begun carving the ark,
paving the way.
That I do not see her in sight.
That the wind no longer hums her name.

That her voice is no longer a familiar taste.
She is a melody,
I'm finally learning
to forget.

Grapevine

 I was reading a novel and a line caught my eye.

As I was reading you came to mind.

It was first year, everything was new.

Dorothy was shocked that your hymen hadn't been broken through.

She said who stays a virgin? Only a prude and

even though that isn't true,

it may have influenced you.

She said you'd have to swipe your "v card" by the end of first year,

because being a virgin past high school was strange and rare.

So off you went looking for someone with a key to spare.

Mark said he stopped in the middle, said he finished in the toilet

because his conscience kicked in.

He remembered his girlfriend.

Funny, how the conscience works,

it kicked in and reminded him of being faithful to his girl, but what ever happened to being faithful to his friend?

The one that lay unconscious underneath him.

Somewhere in between liquid cocaine and Alexander Keith's

I forgot, that consent requires speech.

And even though I didn't rape you

I may as well have,

because I was part of that group that broke bread

with a man who broke through consent.

 I won't dare say forgive me, I'm only human.

Breaking bread with the man who broke through consent,

where's the humanity in that?

When the wolf sinks his teeth into the sheep, if it isn't awake,

does it make a sound?

Does anyone hear it?

Did it concede?

I know it doesn't make much sense

but it wasn't that I didn't believe you.

I just didn't see it through your lens

or even mine.

I saw it, through that of the grape vine.

They say the devil is in the details

and the grape vine planted detailed seeds of doubt.

Well T~T~T iffany wanted~d Mark. H~H~Hounded him for m~m~onths. He fin~ally gave her a~a~a little fun. T~T~The one time h~h~he didn't s~shun her and~nd~d she c~c~cries rape? And Mark is~is~s a good guy h~h~he would never ~ ne

Never say~y~y Never - ~ ~

Is she awake?

I read the line in the novel and my eardrums are distorted,

as my mind is transported

back to your words.

I wasn't awake.

I was high.

I drank too much.

I woke up sore.

The grape vine was blurry

and I was in hurry

as always, to bury the fragments of everything unpleasant.

Until years later when I'm reading a book and I'm reminded of you.

Even though the book is fiction, what happened to you wasn't.

Somewhere in between liquid cocaine and Alexander Keith's

I forgot, that consent requires speech.

Even if a person says yes one million times,

the millionth and one time,

they're allowed to say no.

Half awake means no.

Unconscious means no.

I think I've had too much drink means no.

We should just be friends means no.

I won't dare say forgive me, I'm only human.

Breaking bread with the man who broke through consent,

where's the humanity in that?

Where was the human at that table we were breaking bread at?

There wasn't one.

We devoured your body and inhaled the wine, courtesy of the grape vine

but there isn't any salvation here,

only crucifixion.

We hung you up with attentive ears of the grape vine's fiction.

Forgive me.

I'm only human.

No longer coward.

No longer Judas.

I'm human.

Snap

You're one of three
Canadian world
champions, how'd you
do it?

                        Commitment.

All right, I have that.

Okay let's see what you've got.
You're reciting stop reciting to
me, feel the words, go again. I can
tell you're holding back, again.

You're still holding back, again.

       I can't, it hurts.

          I know, but you have to.

Go back to the moment you
wrote,   you wrote for a
reason right?

To be a champion you have
to go back there and you
have to do it consistently.

Snap

He thinks he's Adam, believes since
she was made from his rib he has the
right to break hers. The VCR and
her back collide like a pedestrian
crossing without looking and a car
running the light.

She screams, I'm sorry.

She looks at me, help me.

Time is frozen. I do not
move.

I'm five.

Snap

Wake up let's go.

                Where are we going?

Shhh he'll hear you.

She grabs a duffle bag and unlocks the
door. My heart is pounding violently.
I'm afraid he'll hear the storm.

Promise we won't go back.

I'm eight.

Snap

What is he doing here?

Mind your business.
I'm doing this for you
guys.

Bullshit
this is for you.

Watch your mouth.
Have some respect.

She grabs the broom, it collides
with my back like VCR did with hers
but I, I am intact. She grabs the wire.
She wears prophet. Spills my blood as
if she can turn it into wine.

I think I'm God.

As if I hold life and death in my
hands I grab two knives. Let the blades
hug my throat like a favorite perfume.

I'm thirteen.

Snap

Wake up.

Why are you sleeping in
class again?

                    I'm tired.

Tired? Or high?

I can smell your friend
again,
is everything all right at
home?

Snap

I'm home. Call me miracle

I'm gliding on these
egg shells like I'm
walking on water.

Tension shoves her down the stairs.
She's lost it, another miscarriage.

I've lost it, compassion.

I found Johnny instead
took a stroll with Alexander
became sentimental with tequila
held her like a nostalgic moment —

40

Why do you hate me so much?

Why? You've ruined me

look at me

look at me.

     Don't you want heaven?

Heaven?

A   heaven wide enough for
you has no room for me
in it.

Respect me   **Snap**

                        I made you

        Snap

            you bastard
  Snap

                you whore
                        Snap

        I should

                have left
            like your
                    father did

    Snap

                        worthless —

42

God why is life so loud?

God, life, is too loud.

But the funeral, inside
my chest

quiet.

A dwindling flame.

A prayer.

A hum.

A lullaby ——

                   This is too
          emotionally draining
                       Ikenna

          I have to get ready
                 for the slam.

Okay, remember,
don't hold back.

              I'll try not to.

Acknowledgments

Firstly, I'd like to thank God Almighty for having my back, always.

My long time friend and creative director Osmosis Jones also known as Fardowsa Abdi, thank you for your support and honest feedback. May we continue this journey of becoming, together.

Jimmy Huynh, my graphic designer, thank you for all of your hard work, professionalism and patience. I look forward to working with you on future projects.

Kali Venianakis, my favourite teacher until eternity. Thank you for being a great teacher, wonderful person, and being awesome with me.

My sister Sara for being my cheerleader, comic relief and occasional camera girl.

Alliyah Riaz, for your support and fantastic taste in fiction, giving me a break from the insanity of producing a book.

Naima Hassan, my friend and fellow writer, for the good times, honest feedback and never cosigning trash.

My friend Luis Mejicano for your aid and providing me with the opportunity to do what I love, teaching kids poetry.

My mentor and friend Mr. World Champion, Opensecret, Ikenna for all of your time, honesty and guidance.

My nieces Neemy and Eman for your explosive diarrhea, projectile vomiting, drooling on me and providing me with the awesomeness of being around you.

Miss Mo also known as Salma Abdulle, for the late nights, laughter, and providing the floor that produced some of my earliest writing.

Ferah Subhani, my sister in faith, thank you for your endless support of any of my endeavours.

To the students that honor me with their stories and serve as a reminder of why I love doing this writing thing:

Amna, Andre, Farhiyah Abdishakur, Ayub Abdulle, Sameera Alkozai , Jasmine Cherry, Jaimie Edmunds, Gaya, Leanne Goulet, Farial Hassan, Alice Jaxon, Baviethan Kumaran, Matthew, Mahee Shirazum, Brooklyn Zaremba.

Lastly, I'd like to thank the Toronto Poetry Slam clan for embracing all the wandering souls stumbling their way onto the stage. Special thanks to: Trevor Abes, Cathy Charlie Petch, David Silverberg and Tanya Neumeyer for being great people.

About the author:

Transient is an overgrown goofball and avid proponent of all things coffee and tea. When she isn't on stage or writing, she can be found drinking coffee, laughing loudly, or inside classrooms conducting workshops on writing and performance.

www.ingramcontent.com/pod-product-compliance
Lightning Source LLC
Chambersburg PA
CBHW030306030426
42337CB00012B/601